HOLY LAND TRAVEL DIARY

A LION BOOK

Copyright © 1982 Lion Publishing

Published by
Lion Publishing plc
Icknield Way, Tring, Herts, England
ISBN 0 85648 483 0
ISBN 0 85648 510 1 (gift edition)
Lion Publishing Corporation
10885 Textile Road, Belleville, Michigan 48111, USA
ISBN 0 85648 483 0
ISBN 0 85648 510 1 (gift edition)
Albatross Books Pty Ltd
PO Box 320, Sutherland, NSW 2232, Australia
ISBN 0 86760 395 X
ISBN 0 86760 262 7 (gift edition)

First edition 1982
Reprinted 1983, 1984, 1985, 1986

Compiled by Eddie Gibbs

Scripture quotations from the Holy Bible, New
International Version: copyright © New York
International Bible Society, 1978

Photographs by Lion Publishing: David Alexander

Library of Congress Cataloging in Publication Data
Gibbs, Eddie.
  Holy land travel diary.
  ''A Lion Book.''
  I. Israel—Description and travel—Views. 2. West
Bank—Description and travel—Views. 3. Bible—
Geography. I. Title.
DS108.5.G49 1985   915.694'0454   85–4554
  ISBN 0 85648 483 0

Printed and bound in Hong Kong

Holy Land Travel Diary

Name
_____

Hotel address
_____

_____

_____

Home address
_____

_____

_____

Passport no.
_____

Introduction

Your visit to Israel will probably be a once-in-a-lifetime experience. During your travels through the Holy Land you will visit many places, not only of natural beauty but of great historical interest and spiritual significance.

This 'Holy Land Travel Diary' is especially designed for your visit, whether you go as a tourist or pilgrim, to ensure you get the most out of the exciting and crowded hours spent site-seeing.

Its handy size means that you can carry it with you for ready reference.

The maps at the front and back will help you locate each of the sites featured in the Diary. The number in each circle refers to the relevant page.

There is a beautiful colour photograph of each place mentioned to ensure a memorable record—just in case your own photo doesn't come out!

Alongside the photograph is an appropriate Bible passage which you can read as you stand on the spot where the events actually happened.

Additional Bible references are also supplied for you to look up at your leisure. These list other important events which are associated with the location.

Space is also provided for your personal record of the interesting things you see and the thoughts that come to you. Jot them down, either while you are on site, or at the end of each day, as a permanent record of your visit. In this way your 'Holy Land Travel Diary' becomes a personal treasury of golden memories.

At the front of the book is a brief history, and at the back you will find a collection of practical information to answer some of the questions already in your mind.

With all this at your fingertips you are all set to make the most of your holiday of a lifetime!

The land and its people

The people of Israel trace their story back to one individual, Abraham, who was called by God to leave his city of Ur of the Chaldees (in what is now Iraq) in about 2000 BC. God promised him many descendants who would become a blessing to the nations, and a land for them to inherit.

Before this promised land (Canaan) became theirs, Abraham's descendants, the 'children of Israel', spent over 400 years in Egypt, first as famine refugees and then as slave labourers. Then God brought deliverance and led them out under Moses. For a generation they wandered the Sinai Peninsula before entering the promised land (in about 1250 BC) with Joshua as their newly-appointed leader.

Following the conquest of the land the tribes descended from the twelve sons of Jacob soon lost their cohesion. Their survival was threatened by the corrupting influence of Canaanite nature religion, and the military threat of local tribes in the surrounding lands—the Moabites, Amorites and, above all, the Philistines. To re-establish law and order, challenge false religion and mobilize the tribes, God raised up local leaders ('judges'), of whom Samson and Samuel are the best known.

The kings

At this time there was a groundswell of public opinion in favour of a king, to be like the surrounding nations. Samuel, somewhat reluctantly, agreed and anointed Saul as Israel's first king. Under his leadership the country gained some victories. But he failed to subdue the Philistines, a warlike people who were a constant threat, and died in battle against them. Saul was succeeded by David who was already immensely popular with the people because of his bravery as a soldier.

Under King David the country increased in material prosperity, military strength and international prestige. He captured the fortress of Jerusalem and made it his capital. Solomon, his son, inherited a large and peaceful empire which enabled him to embark on a major building programme. Life for the people became hard. To support his schemes Solomon exacted heavy taxes and introduced forced labour. Solomon's son Rehoboam was determined to secure his position by making even greater demands on his subjects. His tough line, however, resulted in rebellion and division. The ten northern tribes declared their independence. They chose as their king Jeroboam, who had been leader of a revolt during Solomon's reign.

Two kingdoms

For the next two hundred years (931–721 BC) the nation was divided into two kingdoms: Israel in the north and Judah in the south. After about sixty years of open hostility they entered a period of cautious coexistence. Their disunity made them even more vulnerable to attacks from other nations. Prophets warned both Israel and Judah that unless they renounced the pagan cults which had been introduced they would suffer military conquest and exile. Israel finally fell to the Assyrians in 721 BC when Samaria, the capital, was captured. The population was deported and the kingdom ceased to exist. Judah survived a further 135 years. By this time the Babylonians had won control of the Assyrian Empire. In 601 BC King Jehoiakim of Judah rebelled, encouraged by the Egyptians. Nebuchadnezzar of Babylon sent troops to crush the rebellion and in 598 BC Jerusalem was forced to surrender. The king and leading citizens were taken into exile. Ten years later the puppet king placed on the throne by Nebuchadnezzar attempted to rebel. Jerusalem was beseiged and, after eighteen months, destroyed.

Exile

The inhabitants of Judah were taken to Babylon where they remained for seventy years. Unlike the northern tribes the Judeans retained their national and religious identity. When Cyrus, king of the Persians, overthrew the Babylonians he issued an edict permitting the Jews to return to their land to rebuild the temple and the city of Jerusalem. This daunting task was achieved through the organizational genius of Nehemiah despite much local opposition.

Greeks and Romans

Two centuries later the Greeks became world rulers. Led by Alexander the Great they conquered the entire Persian Empire. When Alexander died in 323 BC at the age of thirty-three the empire was divided up among his generals. Palestine was first controlled by the Ptolemies of Egypt, then after 198 BC by the Seleucids of Syria.

Greek rule brought with it Greek culture. One positive result was the translation of the Old Testament into Greek. But the Seleucid ruler Antiochus IV Epiphanes (175–164 BC) made such radical attempts to promote Greek culture that the Jews rebelled. The Maccabean Revolt, named after its leader, Judas Maccabaeus, succeeded in securing religious freedom for the Jews and, from 129 BC, political independence. Government of the country was controlled by the Hasmoneans—high priests descended from the Maccabean family.

Jewish independence lasted only until 63 BC when Palestine was annexed by the Romans. When Pompey, the Roman general, marched into Palestine he found the country in a state of civil war as two brothers were fighting over the high priest's office. He sided with the older brother, Hyrcanus, and within three months had captured Jerusalem. Palestine became part of the province of Syria and was regarded as a buffer state against the Parthians to the north-east who were never completely conquered by the Romans. Some of history's most famous names were dispatched to the region, including Julius Caesar and Mark Antony.

Under the Romans the Jews were allowed to retain their religious freedom and national leadership. Hyrcanus was confirmed as high priest and ruler. But when the Parthians invaded in 40 BC he was removed from power. Herod, son of Hyrcanus's adviser, saw his opportunity and fled to Rome. The Senate appointed him king of Judea. Three years later, with the support of Roman troops, he was in complete control of the country.

Herod the Great tried to gain favour with the Jews. He initiated several major building programmes. Best-known is the rebuilding of the temple, begun in 19 BC. But the people could not forget he was Rome's ally and hated his cruelty.

Time of Jesus

Jesus was born in Bethlehem, the ancestral home of Joseph, in about 6 BC. Soon afterwards the family fled to Egypt to escape the massacre of babies ordered by Herod who feared a rival king might have been born.

Within two years Herod was dead. Mary and Joseph returned with Jesus and settled in their home town of Nazareth in Galilee. The country was divided among Herod the Great's three sons: Archelaus governed Judea and Samaria until AD 6 when he was banished because his cruelty and incompetence made him no longer acceptable either to his subjects or to the Roman authorities; Herod Antipas ('the tetrarch') governed Galilee and Perea until his death in AD 39; and Philip ruled the territory to the east and north-east of Lake Galilee until his death in AD 34.

Jesus spent his early years in the north, travelling south to Jerusalem only for the annual

Passover feast. Then, when he was about thirty years old, he was baptized by John the Baptist in the River Jordan. Immediately afterwards he spent forty days in the wilderness to the south of Jerusalem where he was tempted by the devil. Following this he began his nation-wide teaching and healing ministry. Much of the time Jesus stayed in Galilee where he made Capernaum his base. Crowds followed him wherever he went but sometimes he managed to escape in order to spend time instructing his disciples and in prayer.

Shortly after Peter acknowledged Jesus as the Messiah, the Son of God, Jesus was transfigured on the mountain. His three closest disciples saw him in his full glory. Then he set off on his final journey to Jerusalem. For some time the Jewish religious leaders, jealous of Jesus' popularity and angry at his teaching, had been looking for a way to destroy him. They viewed his triumphal entry into Jerusalem as the Messiah with alarm and secured his arrest. Pontius Pilate, the Roman governor, bowed to the demand of the crowd gathered in the Judgement Hall. Although no evidence could be found against Jesus, he handed him over to the soldiers to be crucified immediately. But three days later Jesus' followers were overjoyed to discover that he had risen from the dead. Many other people also saw him during the next forty days before he returned to heaven from the Mount of Olives.

The Christian church was born in Jerusalem only seven weeks after Jesus' death and resurrection. Thousands of Jews and Jewish converts from many different countries heard Peter preach and came to believe that Jesus was the promised Saviour. One of the most notable converts of the early church was Saul of Tarsus, the apostle Paul. It was he who spearheaded the church's mission throughout Syria, Cilicia,

Pisidia, Phrygia, Asia (modern Turkey) and across into Macedonia and Achaia (modern Greece). Within thirty years many thousands had become followers of Jesus Christ.

The Jewish Revolt

As resentment of the Roman occupation increased so the resistance movement of nationalists known as Zealots grew. Tension mounted until the outbreak of the First Jewish Revolt in AD 66. At first the Zealot freedom fighters were remarkably successful but when Roman reinforcements arrived the revolt was suppressed with great cruelty. In AD 70 Jerusalem was captured and the temple destroyed. Thousands of Jews were taken to Rome as slaves. The fortress of Masada held out against the Romans for another three years. Finally, rather than surrender, the Zealot defenders and their families committed suicide.

One further major revolt was led by Bar Cochba in 131–35. This time the Jews were completely crushed. Jerusalem was destroyed and rebuilt as a pagan city. The Emperor Hadrian called the new city Aelia Capitolina and forbade Jews to enter it.

Rome's attitude to Jerusalem underwent a profound change in the fourth century. Following the conversion of the Emperor Constantine to Christianity Jerusalem became a holy city. In 326 Constantine's mother, Helena, visited the city to identify sites connected with Jesus' life. From then on pilgrims flocked to Jerusalem.

Enter Islam

Two centuries later, in 614, the Persians invaded Palestine. Once again the land was devastated and Jerusalem reduced to rubble. Shortly afterwards, in 638, the forces of Islam conquered Jerusalem. According to Muslim tradition Muhammad had ridden to Jerusalem on a half-human steed and then ascended to heaven on the horse. So for Muslims too Jerusalem became a holy city. The Dome of the Rock mosque which still dominates Jerusalem was built over the supposed site of Muhammad's ascension.

The Crusades and after

Muslim rule lasted until the eleventh century when Pope Urban II urged Christians to recapture the Holy Land. For over 200 years the city was caught up in a tussle between the Crusaders and Muslim warriors. Jerusalem changed hands several times. Eventually the Crusaders were driven back and the city fell under the control of the Mamelukes of Egypt who ruled the land for the next two-and-a-half centuries.

In 1517 Jerusalem fell to the Ottoman Turks who kept it within their empire until World War I. Suleiman the Magnificent, sultan of the empire from 1520–66, rebuilt the city but following his death it fell into neglect for 300 years.

The Zionists

For centuries Jews scattered throughout the world longed to return to 'Zion', the fortified hill of Jerusalem—symbol of the homeland. Frequent outbreaks of persecution made the longing greater. Then, in the second half of the nineteenth century, Jewish writers and thinkers began to see the hope as a practical possibility. A few groups of Jews emigrated to Palestine and started agricultural settlements. In 1897 Theodor Herzl, leader of the Zionist movement, convened the First Zionist Congress in Basle, Switzerland. After the congress Zionist groups were established all over the world. Their aim was to secure the creation of a Jewish state in Palestine.

By World War I about fifty Jewish agricultural settlements had been established in Palestine on land purchased from Arab and Turkish landowners, often with money from the Jewish National Fund. Known as *kibbutzim* they did much to reclaim barren land and make it fertile. As today, members of a *kibbutz* had little personal property and shared all the tasks. Even the children were brought up communally and were subject to a common discipline. All the members voted on major decisions and were therefore able to direct the policies of their *kibbutz*.

In 1917 Britain issued the Balfour Declaration, largely as a result of the efforts of Chaim Weizmann who was later to become Israel's first president. It stated that the British government favoured 'the establishment in Palestine of a national home for the Jewish people' and that it would 'use its best endeavours to facilitate the achievement of this objective'. At the same time it promised not to prejudice the rights of non-Jews there. The declaration was followed in 1922 by the League of Nations' approval of a British mandatory government in Palestine.

Increasing Jewish immigration antagonized the Palestinian Arabs who held that Britain had promised them the land in return for their support against the Turks in World War I. Large-scale riots broke out in 1929 and again in 1936. Under severe pressure from the Arabs in 1939 the British government issued a White Paper which virtually prevented Jewish immigration to Palestine. Jewish land purchases were to stop altogether, except in 5 per cent of the country, and Jewish immigration was to be restricted to a maximum of 75,000 over the coming five years, then be stopped for ever unless the Palestinian Arabs agreed to it.

Throughout World War II the Jews pleaded for the restrictions to be lifted so that refugees fleeing from Nazi Europe could be given a home in Palestine. After the war, when the restrictions were still not lifted, the Jews took matters into their own hands and 70,000 illegal immigrants—survivors of the concentration camps—were brought safely through the British blockade. British control was tightened but violence in the country became more widespread.

In 1947 Britain took the case to the United Nations. A Special Committee was set up and following its recommendations the United Nations voted that Palestine was to be divided into separate Jewish and Arab states with Jerusalem as an international city.

The state of Israel

In the face of violent opposition from the Arabs Israel was declared an independent state on 14 May 1948. Immediately forces from five Arab states attacked the Israelis. The fighting, broken only by two short truces, lasted until the following year when armistice agreements were signed with Egypt, Lebanon, Jordan and Syria. Israel regained the territory granted her by the United Nations. But Jerusalem became a divided city and Jews no longer had access to the Old City with its holy sites.

Thousands of immigrants flocked to Israel in the following years in need of food, housing and employment. Despite the armistice agreements Arab raids continued. In 1956, when Egypt nationalized the Suez Canal, Israel retaliated, capturing the Gaza Strip and Sinai Peninsula. Although forced to withdraw she was assured of access to the Straits of Tiran and Gulf of Aqaba—essential for trade with Africa and Asia. Nine years later Egypt reimposed a blockade on these vital trade routes. War broke out once again. By the end of this Six-Day War Israel had won control of the west bank of the River Jordan, the Golan Heights, Gaza Strip, Sinai Peninsula and the Old City of Jerusalem. This time Israel refused to retreat.

Israel today

Israel still holds some of the territory gained during the Six-Day War, though in accordance with the Camp David Agreement the Sinai Desert has been returned to Egypt. At present Israel has a population of almost 4 million of which 83.7 per cent are Jewish and 16.3 per cent non-Jewish.

The *kibbutzim* continue to play an important part in land-reclamation and development though some also specialize in manufacturing industries and even run hotels. There are now more than 240 *kibbutzim* in Israel. Less well-known are the *moshav,* another form of collective farming. These fall into two categories: in one families live in their own houses and cultivate their land but buy and sell communally, giving each other help when needed; in the other, land, work and profits are shared but members live independently in separate houses. Both the *kibbutzim* and the *moshav* typify the spirit of dedication which has enabled the state of Israel to survive. The single-minded determination to create a homeland for the Jews has united Jewish immigrants from all over the world despite their widely differing cultural backgrounds.

Jerusalem: The holy city

For Jews, Christians and Muslims Jerusalem
is the holy city. The history of Israel's capital
goes back more than 4,000 years. Its first
mention in the Bible is in Genesis, the story of
Abraham and Melchizedek, who was 'king of
Salem'.

" Great is the Lord, and most worthy of praise,
in the city of our God, his holy mountain.
It is beautiful in its loftiness,
the joy of the whole earth.
Like the utmost heights of Zaphon is Mount Zion,
the city of the Great King.
God is in her citadels;
he has shown himself to be her fortress."

PSALM 48:1 3

The Bible records:
- the city's conquest by King David; his new
  capital   2 Samuel 5:6–9
- the building of God's temple by King
  Solomon   1 Kings 5–8
- the Assyrian siege   Isaiah 36–37
- its fall to Babylon · Jeremiah 39:1–8
- the rebuilding of the city and temple after the
  exile   Nehemiah 3; Ezra 3

- the visit of Jesus as a boy, his triumphal entry, trial and death outside the city walls Luke 2:41-50; 19-24
- the birth of the church on the Day of Pentecost Acts 2

Date

Notes

_____

_____

_____

_____

_____

_____

_____

_____

_____

_____

_____

Jerusalem: The 'Wailing' Wall

The wall is all that remains of Herod's temple
destroyed by the Romans in AD 70. The huge
stones once formed part of the temple
platform. To the Jews this site is sacred. Many
still come to pray and mourn the loss of
Israel's former glory. At night drops of dew
like tears glisten on the stones.

*" Pray for the peace of Jerusalem: 'May those who love you
be secure. May there be peace within your walls and security
within your citadels.'*
*For the sake of my brothers and friends, I will say, 'Peace be
within you.'*
*For the sake of the house of the Lord our God, I will seek
your prosperity."*

PSALM 122:6-9

The Bible records:
- lament for the loss of Jerusalem
  Lamentations 1
- the baby Jesus presented in the temple
  Luke 2:21-38
- Jesus, aged twelve, questions the teachers
  Luke 2:41-50
- Satan tempts Jesus   Matthew 4:5-7
- Jesus predicts the destruction of the temple
  Mark 13:1
- Peter and John heal a crippled beggar
  Acts 3:1-10

Date

Notes

Jerusalem: The 'Dome of the Rock'

This Muslim mosque, built in AD 691, stands on the site of Solomon's and Herod's temple. The area on which it is built is known as Mt Moriah. The great rock inside the mosque is thought to be the place where Abraham was prepared to sacrifice Isaac.

" *God said, 'Take your son, your only son Isaac, whom you love, and go to the region of Moriah. Sacrifice him there as a burnt offering on one of the mountains I will tell you about.' . . . When they reached the place God had told him about, Abraham built an altar there and arranged the wood on it. He bound his son Isaac and laid him on the altar, on top of the wood. Then he reached out his hand and took the knife to slay his son. But the angel of the Lord called out to him from heaven, 'Abraham! Abraham!'*
'Here I am,' he replied.
'Do not lay a hand on the boy,' he said. 'Do not do anything to him. Now I know that you fear God, because you have not withheld from me your son, your only son.' "

GENESIS 22:2, 9-12

The Bible records:
- Solomon's temple built on this site
2 Chronicles 3:1

Date

Notes

Jerusalem: Pool of Bethesda

"*Now there is in Jerusalem near the Sheep Gate a pool,
which in Aramaic is called Bethesda and which is
surrounded by five covered colonnades. Here a great number
of disabled people used to lie—the blind, the lame, the
paralysed. One who was there had been an invalid for thirty-
eight years. When Jesus saw him lying there and learned that
he had been in this condition for a long time, he asked him,
'Do you want to get well?'*
*'Sir,' the invalid replied, 'I have no-one to help me into the
pool when the water is stirred. While I am trying to get in,
someone else goes down ahead of me.'*
*Then Jesus said to him, 'Get up! Pick up your mat and
walk.' At once the man was cured; he picked up his mat and
walked.*"

JOHN 5:2-9

Date

Notes

_____

_____

_____

_____

_____

_____

_____

_____

_____

_____

_____

_____

_____

_____

_____

_____

Jerusalem: Pool of Siloam and Hezekiah's Tunnel

Jerusalem is well sited for defence. Yet its lack of an adequate water supply made it vulnerable under prolonged siege. When threatened with an Assyrian invasion King Hezekiah ordered a tunnel to be cut through the rock to lead water from the Gihon Spring, outside the city wall, to an underground cistern. Work began from both ends, with the triumphant diggers recording their meeting by an inscription on the wall. By New Testament times the rock roof of the cistern had broken away and the pool was known as the Pool of Siloam. Here Jesus gave a blind man his sight.

"As he went along, he saw a man blind from birth. His disciples asked him, 'Rabbi, who sinned, this man or his parents, that he was born blind?'
'Neither this man nor his parents sinned,' said Jesus, 'but this happened so that the work of God might be displayed in his life. As long as it is day, we must do the work of him who sent me. Night is coming, when no-one can work. While I am in the world, I am the light of the world.'
Having said this, he spat on the ground, made some mud with the saliva, and put it on the man's eyes. 'Go,' he told him, 'wash in the pool of Siloam' (this word means Sent). So the man went and washed, and came home seeing."

JOHN 9:1-7

The Bible records:
● the cutting of a tunnel from the Gihon spring
2 Chronicles 32:30

Date

Notes

20

Jerusalem: Garden of Gethsemane

The name 'Gethsemane' comes from an Aramaic word meaning 'an oil press'. Jesus frequently came with his disciples to this secluded garden at the foot of the Mount of Olives. Here he prayed on the night of his arrest. The Romans destroyed the original olive trees—the ancient trees in the garden today are said to date back to the seventh century AD.

"Jesus went with his disciples to a place called Gethsemane, and he said to them, 'Sit here while I go over there and pray.' He took Peter and the two sons of Zebedee along with him, and he began to be sorrowful and troubled. Then he said to them, 'My soul is overwhelmed with sorrow to the point of death. Stay here and keep watch with me.' Going a little farther, he fell with his face to the ground and prayed, 'My Father, if it is possible, may this cup be taken from me. Yet not as I will, but as you will.' Then he returned to his disciples and found them sleeping. 'Could you men not keep watch with me for one hour?' he asked Peter. 'Watch and pray so that you will not fall into temptation. The spirit is willing, but the body is weak.' "

MATTHEW 26:36-41

The Bible records:
- Jesus' betrayal and arrest in the garden
  Matthew 26:47-55

Date

Notes

Jerusalem: Pilate's Palace and Judgement Hall

The public part of Jesus' trial probably took
place in the courtyard of the Fort of Antonia.
Part of the courtyard pavement can be seen
beneath the Convent of the Sisters of Zion.
Games played by the Roman soldiers are
scratched on the paving stones.

*" The Jews led Jesus from Caiaphas to the palace of the
Roman governor . . . Pilate tried to set Jesus free, but the
Jews kept shouting, 'If you let this man go, you are no
friend of Caesar. Anyone who claims to be a king opposes
Caesar.'*
*When Pilate heard this, he brought Jesus out and sat down
on the judge's seat at a place known as The Stone Pavement
(which in Aramaic is Gabbatha) . . .*
'Here is your king,' Pilate said to the Jews.
*But they shouted, 'Take him away! Take him away! Crucify
him!'*
'Shall I crucify your king?' Pilate asked.
'We have no king but Caesar,' the chief priests answered.
Finally Pilate handed him over to them to be crucified."

JOHN 18:28; 19:12-16

Date

Notes

Jerusalem: Church of the Holy Sepulchre

The Church of the Holy Sepulchre stands on a hill which Queen Helena, mother of the emperor Constantine, claimed in 326 was Golgotha ('Skull Hill'), the site of Jesus' crucifixion and burial. The church built by Constantine was destroyed when the Persians captured Jerusalem in 614. Parts of the existing building date back to the time of the Crusades.

"A certain man from Cyrene, Simon, the father of Alexander and Rufus, was passing by on his way in from the country, and they forced him to carry the cross. They brought Jesus to the place called Golgotha (which means The Place of the Skull). Then they offered him wine mixed with myrrh, but he did not take it. And they crucified him. Dividing up his clothes, they cast lots to see what each would get. It was the third hour when they crucified him. The written notice of the charge against him read: THE KING OF THE JEWS. They crucified two robbers with him, one on his right and one on his left."

MARK 15:21–27

Date

Notes

26

Jerusalem: The Garden Tomb

The Garden Tomb is a well-preserved
example of a Jewish tomb from about the
first century AD. It is set in an ancient
garden where an even older winepress and
cistern may be seen. The entrance to the
tomb, enlarged in Byzantine times, would
have been sealed with a large stone. The
tomb matches the description of the one in
which Jesus was laid.

*"Joseph of Arimathea asked Pilate for the body of Jesus.
Now Joseph was a disciple of Jesus, but secretly because he
feared the Jews. With Pilate's permission, he came and took
the body. He was accompanied by Nicodemus, the man who
earlier had visited Jesus at night. Nicodemus brought a
mixture of myrrh and aloes, about seventy-five pounds.
Taking Jesus' body, the two of them wrapped it, with the
spices, in strips of linen . . . At the place where Jesus was
crucified, there was a garden, and in the garden a new tomb,
in which no-one had ever been laid. Because it was the
Jewish day of Preparation and since the tomb was near by,
they laid Jesus there."*

JOHN 19:38-42

The Bible records:
- Pilate places a guard at the tomb
  Matthew 27:62-66
- women find the tomb empty: an angel tells
  them Jesus has risen   Matthew 28:1-7; Mark
  16:1-7; Luke 24:1-8
- Mary of Magdala mistakes Jesus for the
  gardener   John 20:10-17

Date

Notes

Kidron Valley and Mount of Olives

Immediately to the east of Jerusalem lies the deep Kidron Valley which separates the city from the Mount of Olives. Jesus and his disciples frequently crossed the valley on their way to the Garden of Gethsemane. In Jesus' time the Mount of Olives was thickly wooded. It was the scene of his ascension to heaven.

" *Jesus said: 'You will receive power when the Holy Spirit comes on you; and you will be my witnesses in Jerusalem, and in all Judea and Samaria, and to the ends of the earth.' After he said this, he was taken up before their very eyes, and a cloud hid him from their sight. They were looking intently up into the sky as he was going, when suddenly two men dressed in white stood beside them.*
'Men of Galilee,' they said, 'why do you stand here looking into the sky? This same Jesus, who has been taken from you into heaven, will come back in the same way you have seen him go into heaven.'
Then they returned to Jerusalem from the hill called the Mount of Olives, a Sabbath day's walk from the city.' "

ACTS 1:8-12

The Bible records:
- David's escape at the start of Absalom's revolt
2 Samuel 15:23,30
- the destruction of heathen idols in the valley
1 Kings 15:13; 2 Kings 23:4,6,12
- God's glory is revealed to Ezekiel in a vision
Ezekiel 11:23
- Jesus' disciples question him about the end
of the age   Matthew 24:3

Date

Notes

Bethany

Bethany is situated on the eastern slope of
the Mount of Olives, only 2 miles/3km from
Jerusalem. Jesus stayed here, with his friends
Mary, Martha and Lazarus, when he visited
the city. This is the place where Jesus raised
Lazarus from the dead.

"Jesus, once more deeply moved, came to the tomb. It was a
cave with a stone laid across the entrance. 'Take away the
stone,' he said . . .
So they took away the stone. Then Jesus looked up and
said, 'Father, I thank you that you have heard me. I knew
that you always hear me, but I said this for the benefit of
the people standing here, that they may believe that you sent
me.'
When he had said this, Jesus called in a loud voice,
'Lazarus, come out!' The dead man came out, his hands and
feet wrapped with strips of linen, and a cloth around his
face. Jesus said to them, 'Take off the grave clothes and let
him go.' "

JOHN 11:38-44

The Bible records:
- Jesus' return to Bethany after his triumphal
  entry to Jerusalem   Matthew 21:17
- the anointing of Jesus in the home of Simon
  the Leper   Matthew 26:6-13

Date

Notes

Jericho

Jericho is one of the oldest cities in the world. Some archaeologists claim that its history goes back 11,000 years! The flourishing agriculture of this oasis city is dependent on a perennial spring known as Elisha's Spring. Jericho was the first Canaanite city to be captured by the Israelites.

"The Lord said to Joshua, 'See, I have delivered Jericho into your hands, along with its king and its fighting men. March around the city once with all the armed men. Do this for six days. Have seven priests carry trumpets of rams' horns in front of the ark. On the seventh day, march around the city seven times, with the priests blowing the trumpets. When you hear them sound a long blast on the trumpets, have all the people give a loud shout; then the wall of the city will collapse and the people will go up, every man straight in.' . . .

On the seventh day, they got up at daybreak and marched round the city seven times in the same manner, except that on that day they circled the city seven times . . . When the trumpets sounded, the people shouted, and at the sound of the trumpet, when the people gave a loud shout, the wall collapsed; so every man charged straight in, and they took the city."

JOSHUA 6:2-5, 15. 20

The Bible records:
- the rebuilding of the city   1 Kings 16:34
- blind Bartimaeus healed by Jesus
  Mark 10:46-52
- the road to Jericho sets the scene for the story
  of the Good Samaritan Luke 10:29-37
- Zacchaeus becomes Jesus' host
  Luke 19:1-10

Date _____

Notes _____

_____

_____

_____

_____

_____

Bethlehem

In the Bible Bethlehem is called 'the city of David' as it was his birthplace and family home. The prophet Micah foretold the birth of the Messiah here. This prophecy was fulfilled when a Roman census brought Mary and Joseph to Bethlehem and Jesus was born.

"In those days Caesar Augustus issued a decree that a census should be taken of the entire Roman world. (This was the first census that took place while Quirinius was governor of Syria.) And everyone went to his own town to register. So Joseph also went up from the town of Nazareth in Galilee to Judea, to Bethlehem the town of David, because he belonged to the house and line of David. He went there to register with Mary, who was pledged to be married to him and was expecting a child. While they were there, the time came for the baby to be born, and she gave birth to her firstborn, a son. She wrapped him in strips of cloth and placed him in a manger, because there was no room for them in the inn."

LUKE 2:1-7

The Bible records:
- the death and burial of Rachel nearby
  Genesis 35:16-20
- the events leading to the marriage of Ruth
  and Boaz, David's great-grandparents Ruth
- Micah's prophecy Micah 5:2
- the visit of the shepherds and later of the wise
  men Luke 2:8-20; Matthew 2:1-12
- Herod's massacre of baby boys in Bethlehem
  Matthew 2:16

Date

Notes

Hebron

Abraham and his family often camped near the ancient city of Hebron. When Sarah died here Abraham bought the cave of Machpelah as a burial place. The tombs of Sarah, Abraham, Isaac, Jacob, Rebecca and Leah are all in the cave, now enclosed by a Muslim mosque.

"Sarah lived to be a hundred and twenty-seven years old. She died at Kiriath Arba (that is, Hebron) in the land of Canaan, and Abraham went to mourn for Sarah and to weep over her. Then Abraham rose from beside his dead wife and spoke to the Hittites. He said, 'I am an alien and a stranger among you. Sell me some property for a burial site here so that I can bury my dead.' . . . So Ephron's field in Machpelah near Mamre—both the field and the cave in it, and all the trees within the borders of the field—was legally made over to Abraham as his property in the presence of all the Hittites who had come to the gate of the city."

GENESIS 23:1-4, 17-18

The Bible records:
- Abraham's move to Hebron   Genesis 13:15; 35:27
- the visit of Moses' spies   Numbers 13:22
- Caleb's claim to the territory   Judges 1:10-15
- set apart as a city of refuge   Joshua 20:7
- created capital of Judah by David who reigned in the city for seven and a half years 2 Samuel 2:1-4, 11
- the place chosen by Absalom for the start of his revolt   2 Samuel 15:7-10

Date

Notes

Jaffa

Jaffa (called Joppa by the Greeks) has been
Jerusalem's port since Old Testament times.
The apostle Peter stayed in Jaffa after he had
raised Dorcas from the dead. Here he
received a vision of 'clean' and 'unclean'
animals which he soon came to realize meant
he was to work among Gentiles as well as
Jews.

*"At Caesarea there was a man named Cornelius, a centurion
in what was known as the Italian Regiment . . . One day at
about three in the afternoon he had a vision. He distinctly
saw an angel of God, who came to him and said, 'Cornelius!'
Cornelius stared at him in fear. 'What is it, Lord?' he asked.
The angel answered, 'Your prayers and gifts to the poor
have come up as a remembrance before God. Now send men
to Joppa to bring back a man named Simon who is called
Peter. He is staying with Simon the tanner, whose house is
by the sea.' . . .
While Peter was still thinking about the vision, the Spirit
said to him, 'Simon, three men are looking for you. So get
up and go downstairs. Do not hesitate to go with them, for I
have sent them.' "*

ACTS 10:1, 3-6, 19-20

The Bible records:
- timber for the building of Solomon's temple floated down the coast from Tyre 2 Chronicles 2:16
- Jonah's boarding of a ship headed for Tarshish Jonah 1:3
- cedar again floated from Tyre for the rebuilding of the temple Ezra 3:7
- Dorcas raised to life by Peter Acts 9:36–42

Date

Notes

Caesarea

Caesarea was Palestine's first deep-water port, built by Herod the Great and named in honour of Caesar Augustus. The city became capital of the province of Judea and residence of the Roman governors. Recent excavation of the theatre revealed a stone with Pontius Pilate's name inscribed on it. Paul visited the city at least three times before being brought here as a prisoner to be tried by Felix, the governor.

"The soldiers, carrying out their orders, took Paul with them during the night and brought him as far as Antipatris. The next day they let the cavalry go on with him, while they returned to the barracks. When the cavalry arrived in Caesarea, they delivered the letter to the governor and handed Paul over to him. The governor read the letter and asked what province he was from. Learning that he was from Cilicia, he said, 'I will hear your case when your accusers get here.' Then he ordered that Paul be kept under guard in Herod's palace."

ACTS 23:31-34

The Bible records:
- the Christian message brought by Philip the evangelist Acts 8:40; 21:8
- Paul's visits Acts 9:30; 18:22; 21:8
- the conversion of Cornelius Acts 10:17-48
- the death of Herod Agrippa Acts 12:19,23
- Paul's trial before Felix Acts 24:1-25
- Paul's trial before Festus Acts 25:1-12
- the hearing given to Paul by King Agrippa Acts 26

Date

Notes

Shechem

The ancient city of Shechem lies between
Mt Gerizim and Mt Ebal, just south of
present-day Nablus. It features frequently in
Old Testament stories. After the fall of the
northern kingdom in 721 BC Shechem
became the chief city of the Samaritans,
some of whom still live in Nablus. Close by is
Jacob's Well where Jesus spoke to the
Samaritan woman.

*"Jesus came to a town in Samaria called Sychar, near the
plot of ground Jacob had given to his son Joseph. Jacob's
well was there, and Jesus, tired as he was from the journey,
sat down by the well. It was about the sixth hour. When a
Samaritan woman came to draw water, Jesus said to her,
'Will you give me a drink?' . . .
The Samaritan woman said to him, 'You are a Jew and I am
a Samaritan woman. How can you ask me for a drink?' (For
Jews do not associate with Samaritans.)
Jesus answered her, 'If you knew the gift of God and who it
is that asks you for a drink, you would have asked him and
he would have given you living water . . . Everyone who
drinks this water will be thirsty again, but whoever drinks
the water I give him will never thirst. Indeed, the water I
give him will become in him a spring of water welling up to
eternal life.' "*

JOHN 4:5-14

The Bible records:
- God's renewal of his promise to Abraham
  Genesis 12:6-7
- Jacob's purchase of land near Shechem
  where Joseph was eventually buried
  Genesis 33:18-19; Joshua 24:32
- its creation as a city of refuge Joshua 20:7
- Joshua's gathering together of the tribes of
  Israel Joshua 24
- Abimelech's attempt to make himself king
  Judges 9:4
- the rejection of Solomon's son Rehoboam by
  the Israelites   1 Kings 12:1-19
- Jeroboam's fortification of the city
  1 Kings 12:25

Megiddo

First mentioned by the Egyptians in 1478 BC, Megiddo was of strategic importance as it guarded the narrow pass through the Carmel hills on the highway connecting Egypt and Assyria. King Solomon strengthened the city's defences, providing stabling for horses and chariots. New buildings were added by King Ahab who also dug a tunnel to bring fresh water to the city.

"Here is the account of the forced labour King Solomon conscripted to build the Lord's temple, his own palace, the supporting terraces, the wall of Jerusalem, and Hazor, Megiddo and Gezer . . . He built up Lower Beth Horon, Baalath, and Tadmor in the desert, within his land, as well as all his store cities and the towns for his chariots and for his horses—whatever he desired to build in Jerusalem, in Lebanon and throughout all the territory he ruled."

1 KINGS 9:15-19

The Bible records:
- Joshua's defeat of the city's king Joshua 12:21
- Manasseh's failure to drive out the Canaanite inhabitants Joshua 17:11-13
- the death of King Ahaziah during Jehu's revolt 2 Kings 9:27
- the battle between Pharaoh Neco and King Josiah 2 Kings 23:29
- its symbolic use for the site of the last great battle Revelation 16:16

Date

Notes

Nazareth

Nazareth, in Galilee, was the home town of Mary and Joseph. Here the angel brought Mary God's message that she was to be the mother of Jesus. Until he was about thirty years old Jesus lived and worked in Nazareth. After his baptism he returned to the town to begin his ministry but was rejected by the people. Strict Jews scorned Nazarenes as the town was close to several trade routes and these brought contact with the wider, pagan world.

"Jesus went to Nazareth, where he had been brought up, and on the Sabbath day he went into the synagogue, as was his custom. And he stood up to read. The scroll of the prophet Isaiah was handed to him. Unrolling it, he found the place where it is written: 'The Spirit of the Lord is on me, because he has anointed me to preach good news to the poor. He has sent me to proclaim freedom for the prisoners and recovery of sight for the blind, to release the oppressed, to proclaim the year of the Lord's favour.' Then he rolled up the scroll, gave it back to the attendant and sat down. The eyes of everyone in the synagogue were fastened on him, and he said to them, 'Today this scripture is fulfilled in your hearing.' "
LUKE 4:16-21

The Bible records:
- the angel Gabriel's appearance to Mary
  Luke 1:26–38
- the return from Egypt of Mary and Joseph
  with Jesus   Matthew 2:23
- Jesus' early years   Luke 2:51
- the townsfolk's rejection of Jesus
  Luke 4:24–30

Date

Notes

49

Cana

The village of Cana where Jesus attended a
wedding feast and performed his first miracle
is identified by many as Kefr Kenna. A
Franciscan church stands on the traditional
site of the wedding feast. Springs provide
the village with water and sufficient moisture
for fruit trees to grow.

*"A wedding took place at Cana in Galilee. Jesus' mother was
there, and Jesus and his disciples had also been invited to
the wedding. When the wine was gone, Jesus' mother said to
him, 'They have no more wine.' . . . Nearby stood six stone
water jars, the kind used by the Jews for ceremonial
washing, each holding from twenty to thirty gallons. Jesus
said to the servants, 'Fill the jars with water'; so they filled
them to the brim.*
*Then he told them, 'Now draw some out and take it to the
master of the banquet.' They did so, and the master of the
banquet tasted the water that had been turned into wine.
This, the first of his miraculous signs, Jesus performed in
Cana of Galilee. He thus revealed his glory, and his disciples
put their faith in him."*

JOHN 2:1-3, 6-9, 11

The Bible records:
● that Nathanael came from Cana
John 21:2; 1:45-51
● the healing of an official's son
John 4:46-54

Date

Notes

Lake Galilee

Lake Galilee was the centre of a thriving fishing industry in New Testament times. The towns along the lake shore were busy and prosperous. Jesus often crossed the lake to visit different places, but sometimes withdrew by himself into the surrounding hills to pray. Even then crowds followed him, eager to receive Jesus' healing and teaching.

"Jesus . . . withdrew by boat privately to a solitary place. Hearing of this, the crowds followed him on foot from the towns. When Jesus landed and saw a large crowd, he had compassion on them and healed their sick.

As evening approached, the disciples came to him and said, 'This is a remote place, and it's already getting late. Send the crowds away, so they can go to the villages and buy themselves some food.'

Jesus replied, 'They do not need to go away. You give them something to eat.'

'We have here only five loaves of bread and two fish,' they answered.

'Bring them here to me,' he said . . . Taking the five loaves and the two fish and looking up to heaven, he gave thanks and broke the loaves. Then he gave them to the disciples, and the disciples gave them to the people. They all ate and were satisfied."

MATTHEW 14:13-20

The Bible records:
- the calling of Jesus' first disciples
  Matthew 4:18-22
- the miraculous catch of fish   Luke 5:1-11
- Jesus' calming of a storm   Matthew 8:23-27
- his healing of a demon-possessed man
  Matthew 8:28-32
- the miracle of walking on water· Mark 6:45-52
- Jesus' resurrection appearance to his
  disciples   John 21:1-13

Capernaum

At the time of Jesus Capernaum was an
important town on the north-western shore of
Lake Galilee. Jesus made it the base for much
of his teaching and healing ministry. The
ruined synagogue (which dates from about
the fourth century AD) shows a mixture of
Roman and Jewish symbols in its decoration.

*"Leaving Nazareth, he went and lived in Capernaum, which
was by the lake in the area of Zebulun and Naphtali—to fulfil
what was said through the prophet Isaiah: 'Land of Zebulun and
land of Naphtali, the way to the sea, along the Jordan, Galilee
of the Gentiles—the people living in darkness have seen
a great light; on those living in the land of the shadow of death
a light has dawned.' From that time on Jesus began to preach,
'Repent, for the kingdom of heaven is near.' "*

MATTHEW 4:13-17

The Bible records:
- the occasion when Jesus taught and healed
  in the synagogue Mark 1:21-27
- the lowering of a paralysed man through the
  roof of a house Mark 2:1-12
- the call of Levi (Matthew) to be a disciple
  Mark 2:13-17
- Jesus' healing of the centurion's servant and
  of Peter's mother-in-law Matthew 8:5-15
- Jesus' sermon on the bread of life
  John 6:25-59
- the pronouncement of judgement on the
  town Matthew 11:23-24

Date

Notes

Caesarea Philippi

At the foot of Mt Hermon lies the ancient city
of Caesarea Philippi, once a centre of worship
for the Roman god Pan. Herod's son Philip
rebuilt the city and changed its name from
Paneas to Caesarea in honour of Augustus
Caesar. It was against this pagan background
that Peter acknowledged Jesus as the
Messiah, the Son of the living God.

*" When Jesus came to the region of Caesarea Philippi, he
asked his disciples, 'Who do people say the Son of Man is?'
They replied, 'Some say John the Baptist; others say Elijah;
and still others, Jeremiah or one of the prophets.'
'But what about you?' he asked. 'Who do you say I am?'
Simon Peter answered, 'You are the Christ, the Son of the
living God.'
Jesus replied, 'Blessed are you, Simon son of Jonah, for this
was not revealed to you by man, but by my Father in
heaven. And I tell you that you are Peter, and on this rock I
will build my church, and the gates of Hades will not
overcome it. I will give you the keys of the kingdom of
heaven; whatever you bind on earth will be bound in heaven,
and whatever you loose on earth will be loosed in heaven.' "*

MATTHEW 16:13-19

Date

Notes

Some useful facts

Public holidays

The calendar in Israel does not follow the Gregorian system adopted in the West but is calculated according to lunar months. Also, in addition to Jewish holy days, there are Christian and Muslim observances. Information on the actual dates of public holidays is therefore best obtained from your travel agency or the hotel information desk.

The main Jewish holidays are:

Rosh Hashanah	Hebrew New Year
Yom Kippur	The Day of Atonement (Leviticus 16)
Sukkoth	The Feast of Tabernacles (Leviticus 23:34-44)
Simchat Torah	Occurs on the last day of the Feast of Tabernacles when the giving of the Law is celebrated
Purim	Celebrates the Jews' deliverance from massacre (Esther 9)
Hanukkah	Eight day festival of lights
Passover	A week-long festival celebrating Israel's liberation from bondage in Egypt (Leviticus 23:5-8)
Yom Haatzmaut	Independence Day celebrating the Declaration of the State of Israel on 14 May 1948
Shavuot	The Feast of Weeks or Pentecost (Leviticus 23:15-21)

The sabbath

The Jewish sabbath (*shabbat*) begins at sunset on Friday and lasts until sunset on Saturday. Shops and businesses close and most public transport comes to a standstill. In Orthodox quarters car driving is banned, along with anything else which may be regarded as work.

The Muslim holy day is from sundown on Thursday until sundown on Friday.

Shopping

Most shops are open from 8 a.m. until 12.30 or 1 p.m. They then close for three hours, re-opening 4-7 p.m. Jewish shops close around 2 p.m. Friday and remain shut during Saturday. Shops owned by Muslims close at 2 p.m. Thursday and are closed on Friday.

Compare prices before making your purchases and remember that in the markets bargaining is a tradition. Generally speaking things are cheaper if bought where they are made.

Beersheba	Bedouin handicrafts
Eilat	jewellery set with green stones
Nazareth and Bethlehem	olivewood carvings
Hebron	hand-blown glassware famous for its rich colours

Druze villages	basketwork and straw goods
Haifa	factories specializing in the cutting,
Tel Aviv	polishing and setting of precious
Netanya	and semi-precious stones will sell
	direct to the customer

Good buys can also be made in the flea markets in Jerusalem, Tel Aviv, Nazareth and Akko. Look out for leather goods, embroidered dresses and shirts, copper and brassware and Turkish coffee sets.

Remember that there is a 12 per cent value added tax (which may be recoverable when leaving the country) on all items except fresh fruit and vegetables. This tax may not be included in the price of the goods. Look out for the red sign of two men carrying a giant bunch of grapes. This indicates that the business is approved by the Ministry of Tourism. Although prices may be higher, a 15 per cent discount is offered to tourists purchasing with foreign currency. Some stores have a duty free scheme offering a 30 per cent discount on goods delivered to the airport or dock.

Film is expensive in Israel so it is advisable to take a supply with you. The allowance is ten rolls.

Local foods

Menus in Israel have an international flavour reflecting the cosmopolitan nature of its population. Recipes may be Turkish, Greek, Arab, Yiddish and European as well as distinctively Jewish.

'Kosher' food is prepared according to Jewish dietary laws. No shell fish or pork will be served. 'Kosher' meat must be completely drained of blood (animals are killed by having their throats slit) and cleaned with water and salt. In 'kosher' restaurants, milk products cannot be served as well as meat. If you have had a meat course, you will not be able to have milk with your coffee! Listed below are some unfamiliar dishes which you might like to try.

Baklava	a sweet flaky pastry with ground nuts and honey
Blinzes	ham or cheese pancakes
Burma	Turkish dessert made of wheat rolls stuffed with pistachio nuts and soaked in syrup or honey
Chulent	bean casserole
Falafel	a snack sold at stands consisting of spiced deep-fried balls made from chick-pea meal with chopped vegetables and peppers; also sold as a sandwich filling
Humus	puréed chick peas
Kussa mashi	stuffed baby marrows
Kebab	pieces of lamb cooked on a skewer
Lathes	potato cakes
Marak teimara	a dish consisting of meat soup
Mohalabiyeh	a bland milk-and-rose water pudding
Shwarma	rounds of lamb grilled on a spit
Tahina	sesame purée with tomatoes and onions

Banking hours

Sunday, Monday, Tuesday and Thursday banks are open
8.30 a.m.—12.30 p.m. and 4—5 or 5.30 p.m. Wednesdays, Fridays
and the eve of holidays they open from 8.30 a.m. to 12 noon. The
currency exchange desks at Ben Gurion airport are always open.
The Israeli unit of currency is the shekel which is divided into
100 agorot (piasters).

The best exchange rates can usually be obtained in banks.
Hotels also provide exchange facilities. Many businesses quote
their prices in US dollars as well as shekels and payment in a
foreign currency (notes or travellers cheques) often allows
exemption from a value added tax of 12 per cent. It will be
necessary to show your passport when exchanging money.

Post Office hours

Main Post Offices	8 a.m.—6 p.m.
Branch Post Offices	8 a.m.—12.30 p.m. and 3.30 p.m.—6 p.m. except for Wednesdays 8 a.m.—12 noon and Friday, 8 a.m.—2 p.m.

Climate

Israel enjoys a sub-tropical climate. The summer is generally very
hot with the sun shining all day. Rainfall varies greatly according
to the region but is mostly confined to the winter months—
November to February. Spring and autumn are the best seasons
for holiday-makers as temperatures are comfortable without
being too hot. But it can be chilly in the evenings, especially in
the Judean hills.

The hottest areas are those below sea level: the Jordan Valley,
Lake Galilee and the Dead Sea.

Maximum/minimum temperatures

	spring (March)	summer (July)	winter (November)
Jerusalem	52–64 F	66–82 F	54–66 F
	11–18 C	19–28 C	12–19 C
Tiberias	57–79 F	77–99 F	63–81 F
	14–26 C	25–37 C	17–27 C
Eilat	66–82 F	84–104 F	57–82 F
	19–28 C	29–40 C	15–28 C

Dress

Israelis tend to dress casually and light clothing will be adequate
for most times of the year. If you suffer from sunburn remember to
have head and arm covering. Sun-glasses are a must. Pack
something warmer for night-time when the temperature drops.

When visiting mosques and synagogues women should have
shoulders and head covered and not wear short skirts, shorts or
trousers. Men must have their heads covered so cardboard skull
caps are usually provided.

Museums

Jerusalem

Dor Va-Dor Museum
58 Rekov Hamelakh George, within Hechal Shlomo
Specializes in Jewish religious art and artifacts. Open
Sunday—Thursday 9 a.m.—1 p.m. and Friday until noon.

Agricultural Museum
13 Rehov Heleni Hamalka, off Rehov Yafo
On display are farming implements from 2,000 years ago to the
present day. Open daily 7.30 a.m.—3 p.m. and Friday 2 p.m.

Israel Museum
Off Rehov Ruppin
Traces Jewish life and history through the centuries. Open
Sunday, Monday, Wednesday and Thursday 10 a.m.—5 p.m.
Tuesday 4—10 p.m. 'Shrine of the Book' building which contains
the Dead Sea Scrolls is open 10 a.m.—10 p.m.; Friday and
Saturday 10 a.m.—2 p.m. Guided tours on Sunday and
Wednesday at 11 a.m., Tuesday 4.30 p.m.

Rockefeller Museum
Salah ed Din Street, opposite Herod's Gate
Contains a collection of archaeological finds. Open daily
10 a.m.—6 p.m.

Tel Aviv

Bet HaTanakh (Bible House)
16 Sderot Rothschild
A collection of books related to the Bible, manuscripts and
paintings.

Beersheba

Negev Museum
Derekh Ha' atzmaut
Exhibits showing the history of settlement in the region.
Open Sunday to Thursday 8 a.m.—2 p.m., Wednesday
4.30—7p.m., Friday 8 a.m.—1 p.m. and Saturday 10 a.m.—1 p.m.

Megiddo

National Park Museum
Features a model of the city in biblical times and interesting
artifacts. Open 8 a.m.—5 p.m., Friday 8 a.m.—4 p.m.,
Saturday 8 a.m.—5 p.m.

Tiberias

Municipal Museum
Contains a variety of archaeological finds. Open 8a.m.—12noon,
and 5 p.m.

Notes